C#

The Ultimate
Beginner's Guide!

Andrew Johansen

Table of Contents

Introduction

I want to thank you and congratulate you for purchasing this book…

C#: The Ultimate Beginner's Guide!

This book will explain the fundamental aspects of the C# language. It will teach you the tools and techniques that you can use in creating your own C# programs. If you are looking for a comprehensive guide for the C# language, this is the book that you need.

By reading this book, you will learn the basic concepts of the C# language and object-oriented programming. You will also discover the computer framework that you need to install before using this language. Then, you will know how to create variables, methods, constants, and classes for your programs.

This book contains screenshots, actual codes, and practical examples. That means you will be able to use this book even if you have never programmed anything before. With this material, you'll master the basics of C# in no time.

CHAPTER 1

The Basics of C#

In this chapter, you'll learn about the basics of the C# programming language. By reading this material, you'll familiarize yourself with the tools, tricks, and techniques that you can use in creating C# programs.

The Things You Need

Your computer should have ".NET," the framework and development kit for Windows computers. Modern Windows operating systems (i.e. Windows Vista, Windows 7, Windows 8, and Windows 10) have .NET as a preinstalled framework. Thus, if you are using Windows 7, you don't have to install any additional software.

If your computer doesn't have .NET, you can download it for free. Simply visit the official website of Microsoft (i.e. www.microsoft. com) and search for the said framework.

Important Note: If you are using a Mac, UNIX, or Linux computer, you need to get Mono Project instead. This development kit will provide you with everything you need in order to create C# programs (e.g. compiler, classes, library, .NET runtime, etc.). You may visit the www.mono-project.com website to get the framework or get more information about it.

C# – A Powerful Language

According to computer experts, C# is the best programming language for Windows computers. It is perfectly compatible with the .NET framework and it allows Windows users to write programs without downloading any software. This language offers power, flexibility and simplicity. If you're an inexperienced programmer, this is the ideal language for you.

Similar to the Java language, C# doesn't support code pointers or "multiple inheritance." Instead, it offers memory collection and type checking. Additionally, C# has the most powerful features of C++ (e.g. enumerations, overloading, preprocessor directives, etc.).

Creating Your First C# Program

In this part of the book, you'll write a basic computer program. Despite its simplicity, this exercise will teach you how to create, compile, and run a C# program. Follow the steps given below:

1. Launch your favorite text editor. If you're using a Windows computer, you may use Notepad. If your computer runs on Linux, however, you may launch "vi" or "vim."

2. Type this code:

```
class FirstProgram
{
        static void Main()
        {
                Console.WriteLine("The C# language is
awesome.");
        }
}
```

3. Save the file as "FirstProgram.cs". Basically, you should use the ".cs" extension when writing source codes using the C# language.

4. Access your command prompt and type:

```
csc FirstProgram.cs
```

After issuing that command, the C# compiler installed in your computer will process the .cs file. This will create a .exe file in the same location as the source code. For instance, if you saved the .cs file in your desktop, you'll see a program named "FirstProgram.exe" in that directory.

Important Note: The command prompt will display an error message if there's a problem with the source code.

5. Run the application by entering "FirstProgram.exe" in your command prompt.

6. If you did everything correctly, your command prompt should display the following message:

"The C# Language is awesome."

Analyzing the Program

Now that you have created a C# program, let's perform a detailed analysis to help you understand how this language works.

- The first line – This line consists of one keyword (i.e. class) and one identifier (i.e. FirstProgram). Basically, a keyword is a word that has special functions in the programming language. This keyword, in particular, creates a class for your program. A class is a combination of functions and information that you can use in your program. You'll know more about C# classes later in this book.

  The identifier, on the other hand, helps you identify classes, variables, and methods that you want to include in your program. In this example, the identifier "FirstProgram" serves as the name of the class you want to create.

- The third line – This line defines a method (i.e. Main()) for your program. In C#, Main() acts as the starting point of any computer application. Programs start their execution in the Main() method (regardless of their placement in the code).

Two C# keywords precede the method, namely, "static" and "void." Here, "static" informs the language compiler that the method will not create any object within the class. The keyword called "void," on the other hand, tells the compiler that Main() won't return any value.

- The fifth line – This is the final part of the code. It is the line that displays the message on your command prompt. Here, you used a method called WriteLine() to capture a "string" (i.e. a combination of multiple characters) and print it on the screen.

- Just like any object-oriented language, C# accesses the methods and variables of a class using the dot operator (i.e "."). Additionally, C# requires programmers to use braces in identifying code blocks. Lastly, programmers need to end C# using a semicolon (similar to C and Java).

C# Comments

This programming language allows you to write comments in your codes. A comment is a line (or a collection of lines) that gives more information regarding the code block to which it is added. The language compiler ignores these lines, which means comments won't have any effect on the behavior or functionality of your program.

C# supports two types of comments, namely:

- Single-Line Comments – This kind of comment begins with two forward slashes. As its name implies, a single-line comment should be limited to a single line. You'll get an error message if you'll forget about this simple rule. The code snippet given below will show you how to create a single-line comment:

static void Main()

{ // I have a pet. }

- Multi-Line Comments – In some cases, single-line comments are not enough to explain the functions you're working on. Because of this, C# allows you to write multi-line comments. A multi-line comment is a comment that spans several lines. It begins with "/*" and ends with "*/". Here's an example:

static void Main()
{
/ The C# compiler*
will ignore
*this code block. */*
}

The Things You Should Keep In Mind

- A C# program exists inside a class.

- Each C# program starts its execution in the method called Main().

- This programming language is case-sensitive. Thus, class and CLASS are two different things.

- The compiler ignores "whitespaces" (i.e. newlines, spaces, and tab characters). You can use whitespaces freely while writing your codes. Check the following sample:

static   void   Main()
{ WriteLine("This is just a sample.");
}
- C# allows you to use any name for your programs. Additionally, the class identifier and the program's name

don't have to be identical.

- Your program can contain several Main() methods.

- You should use curly braces (i.e. { }) to define the boundaries of a class or method.

- The C# language supports two types of comments: single-line and multi-line.

- You can add a string and an argument to your Main() method.

CHAPTER 2

The Data Types and Variables of C#

This chapter focuses on the data types and variables available in C#. Study this material carefully as it can help you become a skilled computer programmer.

Data Types

C# experts divide data types into two categories: value types and reference types. When working with a value type, you should pass the data to the method you're using. Reference types, on the other hand, simply add a reference into the method (i.e. The value is stored elsewhere.).

Here are the data types that you'll encounter while using C#:

- Byte

- Short

- Sbyte

- Ushort

- Int

- Uint

- Float

- Long

- Double

- Ulong

- Bool – When using this type, the values that you can store are limited to two. These values are "true" and "false". This data type is ideal for logical expressions and conditional statements.

- Char – This data type can hold a single character. While writing a char value, you need to enclose it in single quotes (e.g. 't', '1', 'g', etc.).

- Decimal

Variables

During execution, a computer program stores data temporarily. Programmers use the term "variables" when referring to the memory location that holds the stored data. Thus, a variable has a corresponding value and data type.

In the C# language, you can create (i.e. declare) variables using the following syntax:

<data_type> <name_of_variable>;

For instance: *char x;*

The line given above will reserve a certain part of computer memory to hold a char value. Then, the programmer can access that variable using its identifier (i.e. x). C# allows you to initialize variables during the declaration. The term "initialization" refers to the process of assigning an initial value to a variable during its creation. You just have to use the assignment operator (i.e. "=") and indicate the value you want to assign. Here are some examples:

char sample = '5';

bool isItDelicious = false;

int year = 2016;

Additionally, you can declare multiple variables in a single statement if they belong to the same data type. You just have to separate the entries using commas. Check the examples below:

int test = 1, example = 100, extra = 1000;

char ant = 'a', bull = 'b', cat = 'c';

Just like any programming language, C# requires you to declare variables before accessing them. This language also implements a rule called "definite assignment." According to this rule, you need to initialize a local variable (i.e. a variable written inside a method) before using it. That means you have to assign an initial value to a local variable during its declaration.

Important Note: Variables are named as such because the values they store change each time the program runs. Basically, the value that they store depends on the user's inputs.

Constants

A constant is a type of variable that prevents programs from changing its initial value. Thus, the value of a constant will stay the same regardless of the user's inputs. You need to use "const" (i.e. another C# keyword) when declaring a constant. Here's an example:

const char LETTER = x;

Keep in mind that programs cannot alter a constant's value. That means you need to assign an initial value to it during the variable declaration. The sample given below will give you an error message during compilation:

const bool ANSWER;

Important Note: Most programmers use uppercase letters when declaring a constant.

Creating an Identifier

Microsoft recommends the Camel notation when naming variables and the Pascal notation when naming methods. In the Camel notation, the first letter of the word should be in lowercase. If it is a compound word, the first letter of the second word should begin with an uppercase letter. Here are some examples:

payment　　　　　　*totalPayment*　　Variables

mathematics　　　　　*mathSkills*

The Pascal notation, on the other hand, requires you to start the first word with an uppercase letter. The initial letter of the additional words should be in uppercase too. Check the samples given below:

WriteLine()　　　　　*ReadLine()*　　　Methods

Start()　　　　　　　*Main()*

You can also use numbers and the underscore character in creating identifiers. However, identifiers cannot start with a number. For example, sixDogs is valid while 6Dogs is not.

Important Note: These notations aren't mandatory. However, you are advised to use them while writing C# statements. This way, you can achieve cleanliness and readability in your source codes.

CHAPTER 3

The Operators

Operators help your programs in handling values and performing tasks. Without any operator, computer programs will be utterly useless. That means you have to study how operators work and how you can add them into your codes.

In C#, just like in any programming language, operators belong to different categories. Let's discuss each category in detail:

The Arithmetic Operators

These operators allow computer programs to perform arithmetic procedures. Here are the arithmetic operators available in C#:

Important Note: Let's assume that x = 10; and y = 20.

- "+" – This is known as the "addition operator." Use it to add the value of two operands. For example, x + y = 30.

- "-" – Programmers refer to this symbol as the "subtraction operator." It allows you to subtract the value of the right-hand operand from that of the left-hand operand. For instance, y – x = 10.

- "*" – With this operator, you can multiply the value of two operands. For example, x * y = 200.

- "/" – This operator allows you to divide the value of the left-hand operand by that of the right-hand operand. Here's an example: y / x = 2.

- "%" – C# users call this the "modulo" or "remainder" operator. It divides the value of the left-hand operand by that of the right-hand operand and returns the remainder. For example: 10 % 3 = 1.

- "++" – This is known as the "increment" operator. It increases the value of an operand by one. Thus, ++x = 11.

- "--" – Programmers refer to this as "decrement" operator. It decreases the value of an operand by one. For example, ==y = 19.

Important Note: The increment and decrement operators are unary. That means they can be used on a single operand. Additionally, you can add these operators either before or after the operand you're working on. In the examples given above, x++ and y-- will give the same results.

The code given below shows you how to add arithmetic operators in your codes.

```
class Example
{
        // This basic program will show you how arithmetic operators
work.
        static void Main()
        {
        int f = 3, g = 4;              // This line declares two
                                       variables, f and g.
        sampleSum = f + g;             // This will give you 7.
        sampleDifference = g – f;      // This will give you 1.
        sampleProduct = f * g;         // This will give you 12.
        sampleQuotient = g / f;        // This will give you 1.3
        sampleModulo = g % f;          // This will give you 1.
        f++;                           // This will give you 4.
```

```
        --g;                    // This will give you 3.
      }
}
}
```

The Assignment Operators

As its name implies, an assignment operator lets you assign a value to a variable. Here are the assignment operators that you can use in C#:

"=" – This operator allows you to perform a "simple assignment" operation. It will just assign the specified value to the variable you're working on. For example, the expression *int sample = 100* simply assigns 100 to the int variable named "sample". It doesn't perform extra processes on the variable or the value involved.

"+=" – This is the "additive assignment operator." It adds up the values of two operands and assigns the sum to the left-hand operand.

"-=" – Programmers refer to this symbol as the "subtractive assignment operator." It subtracts the value of the right-hand operand from that of the left-hand operand and assigns the difference to the left-hand operand.

"*=" – This operator, known as the "multiplicative assignment operator," multiplies the values of both operands and assigns the product to the left-hand operand.

"/=" – This is the division assignment operator. It divides the value of the left-hand operand by that of the right-hand operand and assigns the quotient to the left-hand operand.

"%=" – Programmers use the term "modulo assignment operator" when referring to this symbol. You can use this operator to perform a modulo operation on two variables and assign the result to the left-hand variable.

Important Note: When using any assignment operator, make sure that both of the operands belong to the same data type. If the operands are incompatible, your program will display unexpected and/or undesirable behaviors during runtime.

The Relational Operators

These operators allow you to compare the values of two operands. Because of that, they are ideal for conditional statements. Here are the relational operators that you'll encounter in C#:

Important Note: Let's assume that d = 100 and e = 200.

- "==" – This operator allows you to check the equality of two values. If the values are equal, the operand will give you true; otherwise, it will give you false. For example, "d == e" evaluates to false.

- "!=" – With this operator, you can test the inequality of two values. If the values are not equal, it will give you true. For instance, "e != d" results in true.

- ">" – You can use this operator to check whether the value of the left-hand operand is greater than that of the right-hand operand. If it is, the operator will give you true. For instance, "d > e" evaluates to false.

- "<" – Programmers refer to this as the "less than" operator. It allows you to check whether the value of the left-hand operand is less than that of the right-hand operand. If yes, you will get true. For example, "d < e" will give you true.

- ">=" – This operator will give you true if the value of the left-hand operand is greater than or equal to that of the right-hand operand. Otherwise, it will give you false. For instance, "e >= d" evaluates to true.

- "<=" – With this operator, you'll get true if the left-hand operand's value is less than or equal to that of the right-hand operand. For example, "d <= e" will give you true.

Important Note: When using a relational operator, the result that you will get is always a Boolean value (i.e. true or false). Additionally, make sure that you are using two equal signs while using the equality operator. Keep in mind that "=" assigns a value to a variable. Thus, if you'll get confused between the assignment operator (i.e. "=") and the equality operator (i.e. "=="), your program will produce errors or undesirable results.

The Logical Operators

A logical (also called Boolean) operator accepts two Boolean values to produce a new Boolean value. C# supports four logical operators.

Important Note: Let's assume that c = true, d = true, and c = false.

- "&&" – This operator is called Logical AND. It will only give you true if both operands are true. For example, "d && c" evaluates to false.

- "||" – Programmers refer to this operator as Logical OR. This operator will give you true if at least one of the operands is true. Thus, c || e results to true.

- "^" – This operator, known as Logical Exclusive OR, will give you true if one of the operands is true. If both operands are true or false, this operator will give you false.

- "!" – With this operator, you can reverse the value of a Boolean variable. For example, "!d" evaluates to false.

Some programmers refer to "&&" and "||" as short-circuit operators. That's because they can give an accurate result even without checking the entire Boolean expression. For example, since && requires two "trues", it will give you false if the first operand is already false. It won't check the second operand anymore. The Logical OR operator, on the other hand, will give you true if the first operand is already true. It will terminate the process since its condition has already been met.

The Bitwise Operators

A bitwise operator works like a logical operator. The only difference is that a bitwise operator takes binary values to produce a Boolean result. Since a bitwise operator works on binary data (i.e. values that are composed of ones and zeros), they show the result by placing either "1" or "0" in their output.

The C# language supports the following bitwise operators:

Important Note: Let's assume that g = 1, h = 1, i = 0, and j = 0.

- "&" – This operator is known as Bitwise AND. It assigns "1" to the positions where both operands have "1". For example, "g & h" will give you "1".

- "|" – Programmers refer to this operator as "Bitwise OR." It assigns 1 to the positions where at least one operand has 1. For instance, "h | i" will give you 1.

- "^" – The Exclusive OR operator also works for binary data. Just like in Logical values, this operator will give you 1 in positions where only one of the operands has 1. For example, "g ^ j" will give you 1.

- "~" – This is called the "Bitwise Negation" operator. It reverses the value of a binary data. For example, "~i" evaluates to 1.

CHAPTER 4

The Conditional Statements of C#

Conditional statements help programmers in creating powerful and flexible applications. In fact, condition testing has always been treated as an important part of writing computer programs. If you want to be an effective C# programmer, you need to master conditional statements.

If

Programmers consider this as the basic conditional statement of C#. It allows your programs to behave according to the user's inputs. The syntax of an "if" statement is:

if (The Boolean expression)
> *{*
> *The statement/s you want to run*
> *}*

This syntax consists of three parts, namely:

- The "if" keyword – This part informs the language compiler that you are creating an "if" statement.

- The Boolean expression – This portion of the syntax determines whether the program will run the "body" or not. In C#, you cannot use "int" and "char" values for this expression.

- The statement/s you want to run – This part, also known as the "body," is composed of one or more C# statements. The program will execute these statements if the result of the Boolean expression is "true." If the result is false, however, the program will ignore the "body" and pass the control to the succeeding C# statements.

The following example will show you how "if" statements work:

if (x > 0)
> *{*
> *Console.Write("The value is positive.");*
> *}*

In this example, the program will print "The value is positive." on the screen ONLY IF x is greater than zero. If this expression evaluates to false, the program will ignore the Console.Write statement completely.

If Else

The C# language supports "else", a clause that you can add to your "if" statements. The syntax of an "if else" statement is:

if (The Boolean expression)
> *{ The statement/s you want to run if the result is true;*
> *}*
> *else*
>> *{ The statement/s you want to run if the result is false;*
>> *}*

This kind of conditional statement has five parts, namely:

- The "if" keyword – With this keyword, you are informing the C# compiler that you are creating a conditional statement.

- The Boolean expression – This C# expression should result in a Boolean value. If this expression evaluates to true, the program will run the first body of the conditional statement.

- The first "body" – This is a statement or a group of statements that will run if the Boolean expression results in "true".

- The "else" keyword – This keyword informs the C# compiler about the existence of an "else" clause. This part of the statement runs if the Boolean expression is false.

- The second "body" – Similar to the first "body," this part of the code can be a single statement or a set of statements.

As you can see, an "if else" statement is much more powerful than an "if" statement as the former gives you more control over your program.

The code snippet given below will show you how "if else" statements work:

```
if (x > 0)
    {
    Console.Write("The value is positive.");
    }
    else
        {
        Console.Write("The value is less than or equal to
zero.")
        }
```

Here, the body of the "else" clause will only run if the Boolean expression evaluates to false. Thus, the program will ignore this part if the evaluation is true.

Nested Conditional Statements

C# allows you to write an "if" statement within another "if" statement. This process, which is called "nesting," can help you create complex programs that rely on chained conditions. If you'll use this functionality with "if-else" statements, each "else" clause points to the "if" clause that comes before it. Keep this rule in mind—you'll encounter compile-time and syntax errors if you'll make a mistake in writing nested conditional statements.

According to C# experts, your nested statements should be limited to three levels. If you'll exceed the three-level limit, your codes will be complex and confusing.

The code given below will show you how to nest a conditional statement:

```
double r = 50;
double s = 60;
if (r == s)
{
        System.Console.WriteLine("These numbers are equal.");
}
else
{
        if (r > s)
        {
        System.Console.WriteLine("The value of the first variable is greater than that of the second one.");
        }
        else
        {
        System.Console.WriteLine(The value of the second variable is greater than that of the first one.");
        }
}
```

Switch-Case

Switch-case statements execute codes according to the result of an expression. Often, C# programmers use integer values when working with this conditional statement. To create a switch-case statement, you should use the following syntax:

```
switch (value_selector)
```

```
{
    case integer1;
            the statements you want to execute;
            break;
    case integer2;
            the statements you want to execute;
            break;
    //...
    default:
            the statements you want to execute;
            break;
}
```

This syntax consists of the following parts:

- The "switch" keyword – This keyword informs the compiler that the program has a switch-case statement.

- The value selector – This is an expression that generates a value. In C#, the value should be compatible with the comparison operators. Your program will compare this value against the cases listed inside the switch-case statement.

- The "case" – Basically, a case is a label used by the program in performing comparisons. If a case matches the value from the selector, its statements will run. The program will check each case until a match is found.

- The executable statements – These are the statements that you want to run based on the appropriate case. It can be a single statement or a group of statements.

- The break keyword – This keyword terminates the body of a switch structure. As you can see, you need to place this keyword on every case statement that you'll create.

- The default clause – Consider this part as a "catch-all" mechanism. It will run if the value generated by the selector doesn't match any of the listed case labels. With this clause, you can make sure that your program will have an answer regardless of the user's inputs.

CHAPTER 5

How to Create and Use Objects

This chapter will focus on two programming concepts: objects and classes. Here, you will learn how to access the classes present in the .NET programming framework. Read this material carefully as it contains valuable information that can help you master C# quickly and easily.

Objects and Classes

Programming has experienced huge growth during the past few years. This growth has an incredible effect on how modern programmers create computer applications. According to C# experts, OOP (Object-Oriented Programming) is one of the biggest ideas to be developed in the world of IT. In this part of the book, you'll learn how OOP works and how it can help you in creating awesome programs.

Object-Oriented Programming

Basically, object-oriented programming is a style of programming that relies on objects. OOP gives you a programming model that is based on how things work in the real world. With this approach, you'll be able to solve programming problems using logic and intuition.

Objects

Programmers use digital "objects" to represent abstract ideas or physical objects (e.g. cars, books, pens, etc.). While using OOP, you need to remember that objects have two characteristics, namely:

- State – This characteristic defines an object. The definition can be specific or general.

- Behavior – This characteristic declares the actions that the object can do.

To help you understand these characteristics, let's apply them on an actual object—a motorcycle. The state of the motorcycle will define its make, color and size. Its behavior, however, is "moving."

In object-oriented programming, you'll combine information and the techniques for processing them into one. A programming object corresponds to an actual one and holds actions and information.

Classes

In C#, classes define the characteristics of an object. They provide you with a structure for object utilization or a model for defining an object's nature. According to programming experts, classes serve as the foundation of OOP and are closely linked to objects. Additionally, each object represents one particular class.

Let's assume that we are working with a class named "Vehicle" and an object named "Motorcycle". Here, "Motorcycle" is just a single instance of the "Vehicle" class. "Vehicle" defines the state and behavior of all vehicles while Motorcycle is a vehicle.

Classes add modularity and simplicity to computer programming. The information they contain should be meaningful to everyone, even to people who are not programmers. For example, the class named "Vehicle" cannot contain HTTP as one of its characteristics since the latter cannot be possibly linked to the former.

Behavior and Attributes

Classes define an object's behavior (the actions that the object can perform) and attributes (also known as characteristics). Attributes appear as variables in the body of the class. The behavior, on the other hand, is defined by the methods within that class.

If you will apply these on the Vehicle class, you will get "make" and "size" as attributes. Then, the methods that you will use are "move()" and "stop()".

How to Use Classes in Your Programs

In C#, you should define each of your classes using the "class" keyword. After typing "class", you need to indicate the identifier you want to use as well as the methods and variables you want to place inside the new class. A C# class can have the following parts:

- Fields – These are variables that belong to a particular data type.

- Methods – You can use methods to manipulate data.

- Properties – In C#, "properties" enhance the functionality of the "fields." A property provides extra information management abilities to a field. You'll learn about this topic in a later chapter.

The following sample contains all of the parts discussed above. The name of this class is "Book" and it has two properties: type and size. Here, you will know how to define fields, methods, and properties.

```
public class Book
{
        private string bookType;
        private string size;
        public string BookType
        {
        get
        {
        return this.bookType;
        }
        set
        {
```

```
        this.bookType = value;
}
}
public string Size
{
    get
    {
    return this.size;
    }
    set
    {
    this.size = value;
    }
}
public Book()
{
this.bookType = "Dictionary";
this.size = "large";
}
public Book(string bookType, string size)
{
this.bookType = bookType;
this.size = size;
}
public void Sample()
{
Console.WriteLine(" Is this a {0}, bookType);
```

In this example, the class named Book defines two properties, namely, Size and BookType. These properties hide their values inside the fields named "size" and "bookType". Additionally, the code snippet declares two constructors for generating an instance of the Book class. Lastly, this code creates a method called "Sample()".

After creating a class, you will be able to use it for your C# programs. The code given below shows you how to use a class when writing codes:

```
static void Main()
{
        Book firstBook = new Book();
        firstBook.BookType = "Dictionary";
        firstBook.Sample();


        Cat secondBook = new Book("Bible", "small");
        secondBook.Sample();
        Console.WriteLine("That is a {1} {0}.", secondBook.
BookType, secondBook.Size;
}
```

The System Classes

The C# language has built-in standard libraries. These libraries contain default classes such as String, Math, and Console. As a C# user, you need to keep in mind that standard libraries are compatible with any .NET application.

The .NET framework has a preinstalled library that contains numerous classes. These classes help you accomplish basic programming tasks such as networking, execution, and text processing.

You should know that classes hide their logical implementation inside them. As a programmer, you should focus on what classes can do, not on how they do it. For that reason, most of the built-in classes of C# are not viewable. This "principle of abstraction" is a fundamental part of object-oriented programming.

Important Note: You'll learn more about the built-in classes in a later chapter. For now, you will learn how to create your own objects.

How to Create and Use an Object

In this part of the book, you'll learn how to create and use objects for your C# programs. Here, you will use the preinstalled classes of the .NET framework.

Creating an Object

You need to use the "new" keyword when creating an object using an existing class. Usually, programmers assign a new object to a variable that belongs to the same data type as the object's class. Keep in mind that this assignment procedure doesn't copy the object onto the variable. Rather, the variable only contains a reference to the object assigned to it. The following code snippet will show you how it works:

Book someBook = new Book();

This example assigns the new instance of the Book class to a variable named "someBook". As you can see, the "someBook" variable belongs to the "Book" data type.

How to Set the Parameters of a New Object

C# allows you to assign the parameters of newly created objects. Let's make some adjustments to the code snippet you've seen earlier:

Book someBook = new Book("Biography", "large");

This code creates an object named someBook and assigns two parameters to it. Because of the adjustment in the code, the object's type became "Biography" while its size became "large."

Whenever you use the "new" keyword, the .NET framework does two things:

1. It reserves some memory for the new object.

2. It initializes the object's data members.

This initialization process occurs because of a C# method known as "constructor." For the code snippet given above, the initial parameters are in fact the parameters of the class constructor.

You'll learn more about constructors later. Since the variables "bookType" and "size" of the "Book" class belong to the reference data type, your computer program can record them onto the object and the "heap" (i.e. dynamic memory).

Releasing an Object

Unlike other programming languages, C# doesn't require you to destroy objects manually. That means you can release all the memory consumed by your objects without having to perform manual deletions. This functionality became possible because of the CLR, a system that comes with the .NET framework. C# users consider the CLR system a "garbage collector" because it releases unused objects on their behalf.

With CLR, your computer can automatically detect and release objects that don't have any reference. Consequently, the memory assigned to these objects will become available. This approach can help you in preventing bugs and other problems.

If you want to release an object, you need to destroy its corresponding reference. Here's an example:

someBook = null;

This technique doesn't delete the object. It simply removes the reference of the object, allowing the CLR system to perform an automated deletion.

How to Access an Object's Field

In C#, you should use the "dot" operator (i.e. ".") when accessing an object's field. To access a field, you just have to indicate the object's name, place a dot, and enter the field you want to access (e.g. *myBook.*

size). However, you won't have to type any dot if the method and the object you're working on belong to a single class. You have to access an object's field to extract value or to assign a new one.

When working with a property, you need to use the "set" and "get" keywords. The "set" keyword allows you to assign a value to an object while the "get" keyword helps you in extracting value from an object.

The code snippet given below will show you how to use an object's property. It will create an object named myBook and assign "bible" as its bookType. Then, it will display the information on the command prompt.

```
class BookManipulation
{
        static void Main()
        {
                Book myBook = new Book();
                myBook.bookType = "Bible";
                System.Console.WriteLine("This is a {0}.", myBook.
bookType);
        }
}
```

How to Call an Object's Method

In the C# language, you need to use two operators: the dot (i.e. ".") and the invocation operators (i.e. "()"). You won't have to use the dot operator if the method and the object you're working on belong to the same class. On the other hand, the parentheses are always mandatory. To call a method, you just have to indicate its identifier followed by the invocation operator. You may enter some parameters between the parentheses if you want to assign one or more arguments to the method.

While writing C# programs, you can add an access modifier to your methods. The C# language supports four access modifiers, namely: protected, internal, private, and public. These modifiers allow you to restrict your calling abilities when working with a method. You'll learn more about these modifiers in a later chapter. At this point, you just have to know that the "public" modifier makes your objects publicly available.

The following example will show you how to call a method. As you can see, this example is based on the code snippet you've encountered earlier.

```
class BookManipulation
{
        static void Main()
        {
        Book myBook = new Book();
        myBook.size = "large";
        System.Console.WriteLine("This book is {0}.", myBook.size);
        myBook.Sample();
        }
}
```

The Constructors

A constructor is a method that runs automatically whenever a programmer creates an object. The main purpose of a constructor is to initialize the data of the newly created object. In general, you won't get any value while using   this kind of method. Additionally, a constructor uses the name of the class to which it belongs. That means constructors don't use random names.

Important Note: C# allows you to assign parameters to your constructors.

Constructors and Parameters

C# constructors accept parameters, just like any method available in this programming language. You can set multiple constructors in your classes. However, you need to make sure that these constructors have different numbers or types of parameters. That means each constructor has a unique signature.

Remember that a constructor runs whenever you create an object inside a class. If the class you're working on contains multiple constructors, you might wonder which constructor will run while you're creating an object. C# determines the correct constructor automatically. You won't have to do anything manually. Here, the language compiler will select the appropriate constructor based on the parameters that you will use. This principle, known as "best match", helps programmers in writing C# programs quickly and easily.

The example given below will show you how to use constructors:

```
public class Device
{
        private string type;
        private string size;
        // A constructor without any parameter.
        public Device()
        {
                this.type = "laptop";
                this.size = "large";
        }
        // A constructor with two parameters.
        {
                this.type = type;
                this.size = size;
        }
}
```

Let's expand that code snippet to further illustrate how constructors work. In the following sample, you will create an object for each constructor. One of these objects will be an undefined device while the other one will be tagged as a "tablet." Then, you'll execute a method called "Process" for each object and check the output. Here's the code that you need to type:

```
class DeviceManipulation
{
        static void Main()
        {
                Device aDevice = new Device();
                        aDevice.Sample();
                Console.WriteLine("This is a {0}.", aDevice.type);
                Device aDevice = new Device("tablet", "small");
                        aDevice.Sample();
                Console.WriteLine("This {0} is {1}.", aDevice.type,
aDevice.size);
        }
}
```

The Static Data Members

The fields you've seen so far indicate the state of the object being used. Additionally, these fields are directly linked to specific objects inside a class. In object-oriented programming, you will encounter special types of methods and fields, which are linked to the class (or data type) and not with the object itself. Programmers refer to this kind of method or field as "static data member" because it is not affected by objects. Moreover, a static data member can function in a class even without any object. In this part of the book, you'll learn about the static data members of the C# language.

When writing a program, you need to define static methods or fields using the "static" keyword. Place this keyword before the field type or the method's value type. C# also allows you to create static constructors. Here, you should place the keyword right before the constructor's name.

Using a Static Data Member

Before using static data members in your source codes, you need to understand the difference between a static member and a non-static member. Here, let's think of classes as categories of objects and objects as representatives of their respective category. In this assumption, a static member shows the status and behavior of the category to which it belongs. A non-static member, on the other hand, defines the status and behavior of each object present in the category.

At this point, you should know how to initialize both types of fields. As discussed earlier, you need to initialize non-static fields while creating an object. Remember that you should complete this initialization process by invoking the class's constructor.

Important Note: You cannot initialize static fields while creating an object. In C#, you can only initialize a static field while your program is already running.

The code given below will illustrate how static data members work. In this example, the program tries to solve a basic problem: it should create a method that runs continuously and increases the value of the output by 1 during each execution. To keep things simple, let's start with 0 as the initial value. This approach, which helps people in implementing uniform numbering systems, also works in object-oriented programming.

For this example, the name of the method is "NextOutput()." This method exists inside a class named "Sample". This class contains a field called current Output from the "double" data type. As its name

34

implies, currentOutput holds the latest value that the method has returned. As a programmer, you want two things to occur inside the body of the method: (1) increase the field's value; and (2) return the new value as the result.

The returned value involved here is not affected by the objects inside the Sample class. Thus, the field and method used by the program are static. Here's the code:

```
public class Sample
{
        // This is the static field. It holds the current output of the
program.
        Private static double currentOutput = 0;
        // This part of the code denies the class instantiation
intentionally.
        Private Sample()
        {
        }
        // This static method takes the new values.
        Public static double NextOutput()
        {
        currentOutput++;
        return current Output;
        }
}
```

You might have noticed that the Sample class has a constructor named "private." Using this constructor may be confusing at first. However, you will be able to master it quickly. Remember this simple rule: you can't instantiate classes that contain private constructors only. These classes only have static data members and are called "utility classes."

Now, let's create a basic program that uses the Sample class:

```
class SampleManipulation
{
        static void Main()
        {
                Console.WriteLine("Let's count:[1...3]: {0}, {1},
{2}", Sample.NextOutput(), Sample.NextOutput(), Sequence.
NextOutput());
        }
}
```

This program prints "1", "2", and "3" onto the command prompt by calling the NextOutput() method three times. Your command prompt should look like this:

```
C:\Users\SARAH\Desktop>SampleManipulation.exe
Let's cound: 1 2 3
```

Important Note: Because the constructor of this class is "private", you will receive a compile-time error if you will create multiple sequences inside this class.

The System Classes of C#

Now that you know how to create and use objects, you are ready to learn more about the system classes of the .NET framework. In this part of the book, you'll learn how system classes can help you in creating new computer programs.

System.Environment

This is one of the most basic classes of the .NET framework. Basically, the System.Environment class contains powerful methods and fields, which can help you in getting more information about the OS and hardware you are using. Additionally, these methods and fields allow you to communicate with the "environment" of your computer programs. The System.Environment class provides the following functionalities:

- It can give you detailed information about the computer such as the number of processors, the name of the network, the OS version, the active file directory, etc.

- It allows you to access variables and properties located outside the program.

In the following example, you'll see how to apply the System. Environment class in your programs. This approach assists programmers in creating applications with topnotch performance. The property called "TickCount" will determine the time required to execute the program's source code. Here's the code:

```
class Example
{
        static void Main()
        {
        double amount = 0;
        double beginning = Environment.TickCount;

        // The program will test this code snippet.
        For (double x = 0; x < 1000000; x++)
        {
        amount++;
        }
        double conclusion = Environment.TickCount;
        System.Console.WriteLine("The required time is {0}
milliseconds.", (conclusion – beginning) /1000.0);
        }
}
```

TickCount, which is a static property of the Environment class, measures the time that has elapsed since the machine was booted up until the method was invoked. The TickCount property measures the time using milliseconds. With this property, you can identify the length of time needed in executing a code.

If you will compile and run the code given above, your command prompt will show you something like this:

```
C:\Users\SARAH\Desktop>Example.exe
The required time is 369 milliseconds.
```

Important Note: In this example, you used two members of two different classes. These members are TickCount (i.e. from the System. Environment class) and WriteLine (i.e. from the System.Console class).

System.String

This class represents string values of the C# language. Remember that strings are similar to the primitive data types of C# (e.g. Boolean, integers, characters, etc.).

System.Math

This class can help you in performing basic mathematical operations. Basically, System.Math contains methods that can solve exponential, logarithmic, and trigonometric problems.

System.Random

In some cases, you need to generate random numbers for your computer programs. Let's assume that you need to get six random numbers between 1 and 49. In the C# language, you can accomplish this task using the class called System.Random and a built-in method called Next().

Before using the System.Random class, you need to generate an object (or instance) inside it. The system will assign a value to that newly created object. Then, you can generate random numbers within the [0 – x] range by invoking the Next(x) method. As you can see, this method can produce a "0" but always generates a number that is smaller than "x". Thus, if you want to get a number between 1 and 49, the expression that you should use is Next(50).

Here's a basic program that produces six random numbers between 1 and 49. This program will complete the assigned task using the System.Random class.

```
class RandomNumber
{
        static void Main()
        {
                random number = new Random();
                for (double sample = 1; sample <= 6; sample++)
                {
                        double randomValue = number.Next(50);
                        System.Console.WriteLine("{0},
randomValue);
                }
        }
}
```

How to Create a Password Using the "Random" Class

The "random value generator" of the .NET framework is extremely powerful. It can help you to accomplish a wide range of tasks. In this part of the book, you'll use the System.Random class to create a strong password. This password is 8 to 16 characters long and contains at least one number, two uppercase letters, two lowercase letters, and three special characters. To create this kind of password, you should use the algorithms listed below:

1. Create a blank password. Then, run the .NET framework's "value generator."

2. Generate two random uppercase letters and place them at random positions in the new password.

3. Generate two random lowercase letters and place them at random positions in the new password.

4. Generate a random number and place it in a random spot in the new password.

5. Generate three special characters randomly and place them in random spots in the new password.

6. The password has eight characters at this point. To add more characters to it, you should insert a random character at a random position in a random number of times.

Let's convert these algorithms into actual codes:

```
class Password
{
        const string UppercaseLetters =
"ABCDEFGHIJKLMNOPQRSTUVWXYZ";
        const string LowercaseLetters =
"abcdefghijklmnopqrstuvwxyz";
        const string Numbers = "0123456789";
        const string = SpecialCharacters =
"~@!#$%^&*()_+'=/|;:.,><?";
        const string AllCharacters =
        UppercaseLetters + LowercaseLetters + Numbers +
SpecialCharacters;
```

C#

```
static Random sample = new Random();
static void Main()
{
        StringBuilder newpassword = new StringBuilder();

// This code fragment selects two uppercase letters randomly.
for (double x = 1; x <= 2; x++)
{
        char uppercaseLetter =
GenerateChar(UppercaseLetters);
        InsertAtRandomPosition(newpassword,
uppercaseLetter);
}
// This part of the code generates two lowercase letters
randomly.
For (int x = 1; x <=2; x++)
{
        char lowercaseLetter =
GenerateChar(LowercaseLetters);
        InsertAtRandomPosition(newpassword,
lowercaseLetter);
}

// This code block chooses a random number.
int number = GenerateChar(Numbers);
InsertAtRandomPosition(newpassword, number);

// This part randomly selects three special characters.
for (int x = 1; x <=3; x++)
{
        char specialCharacter =
GenerateChar(SpecialCharacters);
        InsertAtRandomPosition(newpassword,
specialCharacter);
```

```
        }

        // This part will generate a random number of random
characters.
        double counter rnd.Next(9);
        for (int x = 1; x <= counter; x++)
        {
                char specialCharacter =
GenerateChar(AllCharacters);
                        InsertAtRandomPosition(newpassword,
specialCharacter);
        }
        System.Console.WriteLine(newpassword);
}
private void InsertAtRandomPosition(StringBuilder newpassword,
char newcharacter)
        {
                int randomSpot = rnd.Next(newpassword.Length +
1);
                newpassword.Insert(randomSpot, newcharacter);
        }
{
        private char Generate(string availableCharacters)
        {
                int anyIndex = rnd.Next(availableCharacters.Length);
                char randomCharacter = availableCharacters
[anyIndex];
                return randomCharacter;
        }
}
```

The first part of the code declared several "constants." In the C#
language, a constant is an unchangeable variable that requires an
initial value during its declaration. You have to declare constants

using the "const" modifier. For this example, you used some constants to define a number and several strings, which were utilized multiple times inside the computer program.

This approach allows you to minimize your codes: you don't have to repeat statements anymore. Additionally, it allows you to perform quick changes to your codes without retyping anything. For instance, if you decided to remove the equal sign (i.e. "=") from the list of special characters, you can accomplish it just by working on a single statement (i.e. the constant that holds the special characters).

CHAPTER 6

How to Define Classes in C#

This chapter will teach you how to create your own classes. By reading this material, you'll know how to set the fields, properties, and constructors of a customized class. Additionally, you will know more information about methods and access modifiers.

Classes – The Basics

A class defines the objects and data types that you can use in your programs. An object (also known as an "instance" of a class) contains the actual information. This information defines the state of its container (i.e. the object that holds it).

Classes also describe the objects' behavior. As you know, behaviors are presented as actions that an object can perform. In object-oriented programming, you should use methods to describe the behavior of your objects.

The Components of a Class

Each class consists of the following parts:

- Declaration – This line declares the class's identifier (e.g. *class Example*).

- Body – Just like methods, classes have a single body. You need to define this part right after the declaration. The body of a class is a statement or a group of statements found between a pair of curly braces. Here's an example:

```
class Example
{
// This is the body of the "Example" class.
}
```

- Constructor – This part allows you to create new objects. The code snippet given below is an excellent example:

```
public Sample()
{
// Insert some lines here.
}
```

- Fields – These are variables that you should declare within the class. Programmers also use the term "member variables" when referring to the fields of a class. Basically, fields contain values that represent the exact state of the object they're pointing to.

- Properties – This part describes the attributes of a class. Often, programmers write class properties inside the field of an object.

- Methods – Basically, a method is a named block of executable code. It can complete certain tasks and allow objects to attain their respective behavior. In addition, it can execute the algorithms present in your codes.

The example given below shows you how to create a class. As you will see, this class has all of the parts listed earlier.

```
class MusicalInstrument      // This is the class declaration.
{                            // This bracket signals the start of the
class's body.
        string instrumentType;      // This line declares a new field.
        public MusicalInstrument() // This line declares an empty
constructor.
```

```
    {
    }
    public MusicalInstrument(string instrumentType) // This line
creates another constructor for the class.
    {
            this.instrumentType = instrumentType;
    }
    string InstrumentType // Here, you are declaring a property.
    {
            get { return instrumentType; }
            set { instrumentType = value; }
    }
    static void Instrument()   // This line declares a new method
for the class.
    {
            System.Console.WriteLine("This is a {0}.",
instrumentType ??);
```

Classes and Objects

In the previous chapter, you learned how to create and use class objects. Now, you'll learn more about this technique.

Custom Classes

Before using any class, you need to create an object inside it. You can accomplish this task using the "new" keyword and the constructors present in the class you're working on.

C# prevents you from manipulating objects directly. In this programming language, you have to assign an object to a variable before doing any manipulation. That means you will access and/or use the object through the variable to which it is assigned.

Important Note: To access the properties and methods of an object, you need to indicate the object's identifier and use the dot operator.

More Information About Objects

Each object in the .NET framework consists of two parts: (1) the actual part; and (2) the reference part. The "actual" part contains the information about the object and is stored inside the heap (also known as "dynamic memory") of the computer's OS. The "reference" part, on the other hand, exists in the computer program's execution stack. The execution stack is the part of the computer memory that holds the local variables and method parameters.

For instance, let's assume that you created a class named "Instruments." This class contains the types, names, and sizes of different musical instruments. Then, let's say that you created a variable inside the class and named it "instrument." The "instrument" variable will serve as a reference for an object and will be stored in the computer's heap.

Important Note: If you want to create a variable without associating it to any object, you have to give it the "null" value. The "null" keyword informs the language compiler that your variable doesn't hold any value.

How to Organize Your Classes

When using C#, there's just one rule related to saving customized classes: save your classes in a ".cs" file. Files that belong to this type allow you to define C# classes. Technically, you can save all of your classes in just a single file. The compiler will work fine and you won't receive any error message. However, it would be best if you will save each class in a separate file. This approach helps you in keeping your classes organized. Obviously, you'll experience some problems in finding a certain class if all of your classes are stored in one file.

How to Use a Namespace

In the C# language, a namespace is a set of classes that are logically related. It contains structures, interfaces, classes, and other kinds of information. Actually, a namespace can also store other namespaces. You can combine your classes into a namespace regardless of their location in the computer's memory.

If you want to use a namespace in your codes, you need to add a "using" directive. Most programmers write their using directives in the first few lines of the .cs file. After inserting the directive, you should declare the namespaces that you want to use.

The Access Modifiers

As discussed in the previous chapter, C# supports four modifiers: private, public, internal, and protected. These modifiers allow you to control the "visibility" of your class elements. Let's discuss each modifier in detail:

- Private – This modifier places the highest level of restriction. If an element is tagged as "private", it will be inaccessible to other classes. The C# language uses it as the default access modifier. Thus, if you won't indicate the "accessibility level" of an element, the system will tag it as "private."

- Public – Use this modifier if you want an element to be accessible to all of your classes. The "public" keyword means that there are no limitations regarding the object's visibility.

- Internal – If an element has this modifier, it will only be accessible to files that belong to the same project (also known as assembly).

- Protected – This modifier prevents users from accessing an element. However, it allows descendant classes to use and access the element involved.

How to Declare a Class

C# implements strict rules regarding class declarations. You will surely get compile-time and runtime errors if you will declare classes carelessly. To make sure that you won't get any error, you should use the following syntax:

<modifier> <class> <name_of_the_class> (e.g. *public class Vehicles*)

The Body of a Class

You should write the body of your class right after its identifier. Keep in mind that the "body" is the part that contains the executable codes. Just like other programming languages, you should write this part inside a pair of curly braces.

The "this" Keyword

In C#, the "this" keyword tags the current element (e.g. object) as a reference for the next process. You can consider this as a tool for accessing the contents of a class. Here are some examples:

this.sampleField;   // Use this syntax to access a particular field.

this.sampleMethod(); // Use this syntax to run a method.

this(8, 9);   // Use this syntax to trigger a constructor that contains two parameters.

The Fields

An object represents things in the physical world. To define an object, you should concentrate on its attributes, which are linked to the purpose of your computer program. You need to store these attributes in the class declaration using special variables. These special variables, known as fields, define the status of the object you're working on.

How to Declare a Field

C# requires you to declare your fields in the body of a class. The code given below declares multiple fields:

```
class Example
{
        double salary;
        char favoriteLetter;
        string yourName;
}
```

A Field's Scope

The scope of any field begins from the part where it is written and continues until the end of the class's body.

Initializing a Field

C# allows you to set the value of your newly created fields. The syntax that you need to use is similar to that of ordinary variables:

<modifier> <type_of_field> <name_of_field> = <value>;

Important Note: Make sure that the initial value is compatible with the field you are using. As you know, C# implements strict rules regarding the compatibility of data types. Check the following example:

```
class Sample
{
        int payment = 5000;
        char letter = 'x';
        string[] instruments = new string[] { "guitar", "drums" };
        Vehicles myVehicle = new Vehicles();
}
```

The Default Value of a Field

Whenever you create an object inside any class, the system allocates memory for the fields of that new object. The system does this by setting an initial value to each field. If you do not set the default values for your class fields, they will get the values specified by the .NET framework.

This functionality is the main difference between fields and local variables. The language compiler will give you an error message if any of your local variables do not contain a value.

How to Customize the Default Values

The C# language allows you to set the default values of your fields. With this feature, you can boost the cleanliness and readability of your source codes. Let's use the fields you've seen earlier as examples:

```
class Sample
{
        int payment = 0;
        char letter = null;
        string[] instruments = null;
        Vehicles myVehicle = null;

}
```

Conclusion

Thank you for reading this book, I hope it was able to help you master the basics of C#.

Now, you should reread this book to reinforce your memory and continue writing your own programs. Keep in mind that you won't become a great programmer if you don't practice your programming skills. The code snippets included in this book can serve as excellent guides. It would be best if you will use them as templates in writing your own computer programs.

Finally, if you enjoyed this book, please take the time to share your thoughts and post a positive review on Amazon. It'd be greatly appreciated!

Thank you and good luck!